Angular Routing

Everything you need to know

Abdelfattah Ragab

Angular Routing

Everything you need to know

Abdelfattah Ragab

Introduction

Welcome to the book "Angular Routing".
In this book, I explain everything you need to know about Angular routing.
Routing helps you to change what the user sees in a single-page app.
In this book, you will learn how to implement common routing tasks. You will learn how to set up routes, retrieve route information, display 404 pages, prevent unauthorized access, and much more.
By the end of this book, you will be confident working with routing in your Angular application and be able to handle all kinds of scenarios.
Let us get started.

Configuration

If you open the Angular application in Visual Studio Code, you can find the **app.config.ts** file in the **src/app** folder of the application.

In the `providers` array, you must specify the routes as follows: `provideRouter(routes)`. This is what it looks like:

```
import { ApplicationConfig,
provideZoneChangeDetection } from
'@angular/core';
import { provideRouter } from
'@angular/router';

import { routes } from './app.routes';

export const appConfig:
ApplicationConfig = {
  providers:
[provideZoneChangeDetection({
eventCoalescing: true }),
provideRouter(routes)]
};
```

The `routes` array is defined in the **app.routes.ts** file. It will be empty at first:

```
import { Routes } from
'@angular/router';

export const routes: Routes = [];
```

```
<router-outlet />
```

The router outlet is a directive that acts as a placeholder that Angular fills dynamically based on the current router state.

If you open the **app.component.html** file, you will find it in the last line of the file. Normally we remove all the code above this line when we start a new application. We remove everything in the **app.component.html** file and leave only one line: the `<router outlet />`.

If you want to add a header to the application, you can add it above this line, and if you want to add a footer, you need to add it after this line. The router outlet line is the place where the dynamic component is placed based on the current router state.

How the router works

Angular routing is very simple, you just have to add a new entry to the routes array. That's it.

If you enter this path in the address bar, the desired component will be displayed in the `<router-outlet />` placeholder.

Let us see this in action by adding a new entry to the routes array in the **app.routes.ts** file.

```
import { Routes } from
'@angular/router';
```

```
import { HomeComponent } from
'./pages/home/home.component';

export const routes: Routes = [{ path:
'home', component: HomeComponent }];
```

Now, run run the application and write the following url in the address bar:
http://localhost:4200/**home**

You will find a page saying "home works!", the content of the home page.
Don't forget to remove everything from the app.component.html page except the
```
<router-outlet />
```

Default route

When you run the application, a blank page is displayed.
I want it to default to the home page.
I will add a new empty path to the route array as follows:

```
import { Routes } from
'@angular/router';
import { HomeComponent } from
'./pages/home/home.component';

export const routes: Routes = [
```

```
  { path: '', redirectTo: 'home',
pathMatch: 'full' },
   { path: 'home', component:
HomeComponent },
];
```

redirectTo

We use the `redirectTo` property to redirect from one route to another.
When the user tries to access the base url, `http://localhost:4200`, it will redirect to the "home" entry, `http://localhost:4200/home`, and load the `HomeComponent`.

pathMatch

The `pathMatch` property can take two values: `full` or `prefix`.
The `pathMatch: 'full'` option is crucial here; it tells the router to redirect only if the entire URL path matches the empty string.
If you set `pathMatch: 'prefix'` for the empty path, any route starting with the empty string (which is all routes) would trigger the redirect, which is not normally the desired behavior.

Not Found

Add a new entry to the routes array as follows:

```
import { Routes } from
'@angular/router';
import { HomeComponent } from
'./pages/home/home.component';
import { NotFoundComponent } from
'./pages/not-found/not-found.component';

export const routes: Routes = [
  { path: '', redirectTo: 'home',
pathMatch: 'full' },
  { path: 'home', component:
HomeComponent },
  { path: 'not-found', component:
NotFoundComponent },
];
```

When you visit the URL
`http://localhost:4200/not-found`, the
`NotFoundComponent` is loaded.
You can fill the `NotFoundComponent` with any content
to inform the user that the page they are looking for
does not exist.

Wildcard route

A wildcard route is defined with the syntax `**` in the
routing configuration. This route should usually be at the

end of your route definitions to ensure that only routes that were not found by any of the previous routes are included. The routes are matched in the order in which you define them in the array.

```
import { Routes } from
'@angular/router';
import { HomeComponent } from
'./pages/home/home.component';
import { NotFoundComponent } from
'./pages/not-found/not-found.component';

export const routes: Routes = [
  { path: '', redirectTo: 'home',
pathMatch: 'full' },
  { path: 'home', component:
HomeComponent },
  { path: 'not-found', component:
NotFoundComponent },
  {
    path: '**',
    redirectTo: 'not-found',
  },
];
```

As a final step, I redirect all routes to the `not-found` route.

title

When defining routes, you can specify page titles. It is strongly recommended that you do this as it helps to assess accessibility. If you are using Lighthouse to test your application.

```
{ path: 'home', component:
HomeComponent, title: 'Home - Mini Shop'
},
{ path: 'about', component:
AboutComponent, title: 'About - Mini
Shop' },
{ path: 'contact', component:
ContactComponent, title: 'Contact - Mini
Shop' },
```

Guards

Guards allow developers to control access to routes in an Angular application based on certain conditions.

canActivate

canActivate allows developers to define logic that determines whether a user can navigate to a specific route.
Let us assume we have the "Add products" page, which should only be accessible to administrators.

```
import { Routes } from
'@angular/router';
import { HomeComponent } from
'./pages/home/home.component';
```

```typescript
import { NotFoundComponent } from
'./pages/not-found/not-found.component';
import { AddProductComponent } from
'./pages/add-product/add-product.compone
nt';

export const routes: Routes = [
  { path: '', redirectTo: 'home',
pathMatch: 'full' },
  { path: 'home', component:
HomeComponent },
  { path: 'add-product', component:
AddProductComponent },
  { path: 'not-found', component:
NotFoundComponent },
  {
    path: '**',
    redirectTo: 'not-found',
  },
];
```

Let us first declare the `canActivate` method, which decides whether the user is allowed to access the URL or not. You can call it whatever you want. I will call it authGuard. If you are wondering where to create this method, you can create a new folder"**guards**" inside the app folder and create a new file **"authGuard.ts"** in it.

```typescript
import { inject } from '@angular/core';
import {
  ActivatedRouteSnapshot,
```

```typescript
  RedirectCommand,
  Router,
  RouterStateSnapshot,
} from '@angular/router';
import { AuthService } from
'../services/auth.service';

export const authGuard = (
  route: ActivatedRouteSnapshot,
  state: RouterStateSnapshot
): RedirectCommand | boolean |
Promise<RedirectCommand> |
Promise<boolean> => {
  const authService =
inject(AuthService);
  const router = inject(Router);
  if (authService.isAdmin()) {
    return true;
  } else {
    return
router.navigateByUrl('/login');
  }
};
```

Use it as follows:

```typescript
import { Routes } from
'@angular/router';
import { HomeComponent } from
'./pages/home/home.component';
import { NotFoundComponent } from
'./pages/not-found/not-found.component';
```

```typescript
import { AddProductComponent } from
'./pages/add-product/add-product.compone
nt';
import { authGuard } from
'./guards/authGuard';

export const routes: Routes = [
  { path: '', redirectTo: 'home',
pathMatch: 'full' },
  { path: 'home', component:
HomeComponent },
  {
    path: 'add-product',
    component: AddProductComponent,
    canActivate: [authGuard],
  },
  { path: 'not-found', component:
NotFoundComponent },
  {
    path: '**',
    redirectTo: 'not-found',
  },
];
```

You can protect any path that way.

canDeactivate

The `canDeactivate` guard is a route guard that allows
you to control whether a user can leave a specific route

or component. This is particularly useful in scenarios where users may have unsaved changes or are in the middle of a workflow and you want to prevent them from accidentally navigating away without confirmation.

Resolvers

Resolvers are a powerful feature that can be used to retrieve data before a route is activated. They act as middleware that allows you to load necessary data before the component associated with a route is rendered. This ensures that the component has all the necessary information when it is displayed, resulting in a smoother user experience.

Create a new **"resolvers"** folder and create a new file **"products.resolver.ts"** in it.

```typescript
import { Injectable } from
'@angular/core';
import {
  Resolve,
  ActivatedRouteSnapshot,
  RouterStateSnapshot,
} from '@angular/router';
import { Observable } from 'rxjs';
import { ProductsService } from
'../../services/products.service';

@Injectable({
  providedIn: 'root',
})
```

```typescript
export class ProductsResolver implements
Resolve<any> {
  constructor(private productsService:
ProductsService) {}

  resolve(
    route: ActivatedRouteSnapshot,
    state: RouterStateSnapshot
  ): Observable<any> {
    return
this.productsService.getProducts();
  }
}
```

Use it with our path

```typescript
import { Routes } from
'@angular/router';
import { HomeComponent } from
'./pages/home/home.component';
import { NotFoundComponent } from
'./pages/not-found/not-found.component';
import { AddProductComponent } from
'./pages/add-product/add-product.compone
nt';
import { authGuard } from
'./guards/authGuard';
import { ProductsComponent } from
'./pages/products/products.component';
import { ProductsResolver } from
'./pages/resolvers/products.resolver';
```

```typescript
export const routes: Routes = [
  { path: '', redirectTo: 'home',
pathMatch: 'full' },
  { path: 'home', component:
HomeComponent },
  {
    path: 'products',
    component: ProductsComponent,
    resolve: {
      products: ProductsResolver,
    },
  },
  {
    path: 'add-product',
    component: AddProductComponent,
    canActivate: [authGuard],
  },
  { path: 'not-found', component:
NotFoundComponent },
  {
    path: '**',
    redirectTo: 'not-found',
  },
];
```

In the app.component.ts we can access the products as follows:

```typescript
import { Component, OnInit } from
'@angular/core';
import { ActivatedRoute } from
'@angular/router';
```

```typescript
@Component({
  selector: 'app-products',
  standalone: true,
  imports: [],
  templateUrl:
'./products.component.html',
  styleUrl: './products.component.css',
})
export class ProductsComponent
implements OnInit {
  products: any;

  constructor(private readonly route:
ActivatedRoute) {}

  ngOnInit(): void {
    this.products =
this.route.snapshot.data['products'];

//or

    this.route.data.subscribe((data) => {
      this.products = data['products'];
    });

  }
}
```

Static Data

You can also pass static data to a route, which can be particularly useful in scenarios where you only need to provide read information to the components without resorting to dynamic data.

Static data refers to fixed information that is associated with a route and does not change during the lifecycle of the application. This data can include elements such as: page title, breadcrumb text and configuration settings. Here, we will define routes that include static data for page titles, breadcrumb text, and configuration settings.

```typescript
import { Routes } from
'@angular/router';
import { HomeComponent } from
'./pages/home/home.component';
import { NotFoundComponent } from
'./pages/not-found/not-found.component';
import { AddProductComponent } from
'./pages/add-product/add-product.compone
nt';
import { authGuard } from
'./guards/authGuard';
import { ProductsComponent } from
'./pages/products/products.component';
import { ProductsResolver } from
'./pages/resolvers/products.resolver';

export const routes: Routes = [
  { path: '', redirectTo: 'home',
pathMatch: 'full' },
```

```typescript
  {
    path: 'home',
    component: HomeComponent,
    data: {
      title: 'Home Page',
      breadcrumb: 'Home',
      config: { theme: 'light', layout:
'default' },
    },
  },
  {
    path: 'products',
    component: ProductsComponent,
    resolve: {
      products: ProductsResolver,
    },
  },
  {
    path: 'add-product',
    component: AddProductComponent,
    canActivate: [authGuard],
  },
  { path: 'not-found', component:
NotFoundComponent },
  {
    path: '**',
    redirectTo: 'not-found',
  },
];
```

You can access this data in your components using the `ActivatedRoute` service.

```typescript
import { Component, OnInit } from
'@angular/core';
import { ActivatedRoute } from
'@angular/router';

@Component({
  selector: 'app-home',
  standalone: true,
  imports: [],
  templateUrl: './home.component.html',
  styleUrl: './home.component.css',
})
export class HomeComponent implements
OnInit {
  pageTitle: string = '';
  breadcrumb: string = '';
  config: any;

  constructor(private route:
ActivatedRoute) {}

  ngOnInit() {
    this.pageTitle =
this.route.snapshot.data['title'];
    this.breadcrumb =
this.route.snapshot.data['breadcrumb'];
    this.config =
this.route.snapshot.data['config'];
  }
}
```

Params

We use params to specify information in the URL, e.g. the product ID and so on.

```typescript
import { Routes } from
'@angular/router';
import { HomeComponent } from
'./pages/home/home.component';
import { NotFoundComponent } from
'./pages/not-found/not-found.component';
import { AddProductComponent } from
'./pages/add-product/add-product.compone
nt';
import { authGuard } from
'./guards/authGuard';
import { ProductsComponent } from
'./pages/products/products.component';
import { ProductsResolver } from
'./pages/resolvers/products.resolver';
import { ProductDetailsComponent } from
'./pages/product-details/product-details
.component';

export const routes: Routes = [
  { path: '', redirectTo: 'home',
pathMatch: 'full' },
  {
    path: 'home',
    component: HomeComponent,
    data: {
      title: 'Home Page',
```

```typescript
      breadcrumb: 'Home',
      config: { theme: 'light', layout:
'default' },
    },
  },
  {
    path: 'products',
    component: ProductsComponent,
    resolve: {
      products: ProductsResolver,
    },
  },
  {
    path: 'products/:id',
    component: ProductDetailsComponent,
  },
  {
    path: 'add-product',
    component: AddProductComponent,
    canActivate: [authGuard],
  },
  { path: 'not-found', component:
NotFoundComponent },
  {
    path: '**',
    redirectTo: 'not-found',
  },
];
```

The url will look as follows:

```
http://localhost:4200/products/2
```

The last segment is the id. You can read it in the component as follows:

```typescript
import { Component, OnInit } from '@angular/core';
import { ActivatedRoute } from '@angular/router';

@Component({
  selector: 'app-product-details',
  standalone: true,
  imports: [],
  templateUrl: './product-details.component.html',
  styleUrl: './product-details.component.css',
})
export class ProductDetailsComponent implements OnInit {
  id: any;

  constructor(private readonly route: ActivatedRoute) {}

  ngOnInit(): void {
    this.id = this.route.snapshot.params['id'];
  }
}
```

By injecting an instance of the ActivatedRoute you can read the params.

You have noticed that we can read the params from the snapshot and we can also subscribe to the params changes and you may wonder why we should subscribe. Most ecommerce websites display a list of the popular products at the end of the product details page.

Clicking on any of these products will load the new product, say you are on the page `http://localhost:4200/products/2` and clicked on the product `http://localhost:4200/products/3`

We are on the same page, the product details page, which means that the component instance has already been created and the constructor and onInit function have already been triggered. They are only triggered once when the component instance is created and will never be triggered again as long as the component already exists on the screen. Other lifecycle hooks are triggered, such as `ngOnChanges`, but for `ngOnInit` and `Constructor` they are only called once.

This means that the product detail page will continue to show the details of the first product and will not notice the change.

The solution is to subscribe to the route params, which will notify you of any changes to the parameters so that you can successfully load the desired product details.

The fact that the onInit and constructor are rendered once remains, but it is the subscription that catches the changes and responds correctly.

QueryParams

These are additional parameters that can be appended to the URL after a question mark (?). They are typically used for filtering or sorting data. For example, `http://localhost:4200/products`**?page=2&sort=asc** includes query parameters for pagination and sorting.

Similar to params you can read it in the component as follows:

```typescript
import { Component, OnInit } from
'@angular/core';
import { ActivatedRoute } from
'@angular/router';

@Component({
  selector: 'app-products',
  standalone: true,
  imports: [],
  templateUrl:
'./products.component.html',
  styleUrl: './products.component.css',
})
export class ProductsComponent
implements OnInit {
  products: any;
  page: any;
  sort: any;

  constructor(private readonly route:
ActivatedRoute) {}
```

```typescript
ngOnInit(): void {
  this.products =
this.route.snapshot.data['products'];
  this.page =
this.route.snapshot.queryParams['page'];
  this.sort =
this.route.snapshot.data['sort'];
  }
}
```

In modern applications, pagination and sorting is done
on the backend server and not on the client. When we
call the REST API endpoint to get the list of products,
we send the take, skip and sort parameters and then
display the returned data.
It makes no sense to load 10k records onto the client
and then only display the first 10 records because of
pagination. If that's the case, it would be better to load
only those 10 records by passing the right parameters to
the backend, which saves resources and provides a
better user experience.

RouterLink

`RouterLink` is a directive in Angular that allows you
to navigate between different routes in your application
declaratively.

The RouterLink directive can be used in your templates to create links that navigate to different routes. It can be applied to any HTML element.
Here's a simple example of how to use RouterLink:

```html
<div routerLink="/">Home</div>
<div
routerLink="/products">Products</div>
```

Or

```html
<div [routerLink]="['/']">Home</div>
<div [routerLink]="['/',
'products']">Products</div>
```

The first way is suitable for strings, but you can use the array mode to customize your route. For example, to provide a dynamic value like the id.

```html
<div [routerLink]="['/', 'products',
id]">Products</div>
```

You can provide query params as follows:

```html
<div
  [routerLink]="['/', 'products', id]"
  [queryParams]="{ page: 1, sort: 'asc'
}"
>
  Products
</div>
```

Do not forget to import `RouterModule` if you are using the standalone component.

```
import { Component } from
'@angular/core';
import { RouterModule } from
'@angular/router';

@Component({
  selector: 'app-header',
  standalone: true,
  imports: [RouterModule],
  templateUrl:
'./header.component.html',
  styleUrl: './header.component.css',
})
export class HeaderComponent {
  id: any;
}
```

navigateByUrl

If you want to perform the navigation dynamically from the code, first inject the router service and then call one of the navigation methods, e.g. `navigateByUrl`

```
import { Component } from
'@angular/core';
import { Router, RouterLink } from
'@angular/router';

@Component({
```

```typescript
  selector: 'app-header',
  standalone: true,
  imports: [RouterLink],
  templateUrl:
'./header.component.html',
  styleUrl: './header.component.css',
})
export class HeaderComponent {
  id: any;
  constructor(private readonly router:
Router) {}

  onProducts() {

this.router.navigateByUrl('/products');
  }
}
```

You can also use the navigate method, which takes an array of url segments and options as follows:

```typescript
import { Component } from
'@angular/core';
import { Router, RouterLink } from
'@angular/router';

@Component({
  selector: 'app-header',
  standalone: true,
  imports: [RouterLink],
  templateUrl:
'./header.component.html',
```

```typescript
  styleUrl: './header.component.css',
})
export class HeaderComponent {
  id: any;
  constructor(private readonly router:
Router) {}

  onProducts() {
    this.router.navigate(['/',
'products', this.id], {
      queryParams: {
        page: 1,
        sort: 'asc',
      },
    });
  }
}
```

To call the onProducts method from the template, simply add it to the click event of the button as follows:

```html
<button
(click)="onProducts()">Products</button>
```

RouterLinkActive

`RouterLinkActive` is useful for styling navigation links to indicate which route is currently active. You specify the class name to be applied when the intended path is active. For example:

```html
  <a routerLink="/"
routerLinkActive="active">Home</a>
  <a routerLink="/about"
routerLinkActive="active">About</a>
  <a routerLink="/products"
routerLinkActive="active">Products</a>
```

The active class is applied according to the current active path. If you are on the `http://localhost:4200/products` page, the "Products" item is highlighted and so on.
It will match all subpages, which means that the "Products" element will be highlighted when you visit a subpage like `http://localhost:4200/products/2`. If you want an exact match without sub-routes, you should specify this in the `RouterLinkActiveOptions`. For example:

```html
  <a
    routerLink="/products"
    routerLinkActive="active"
    [routerLinkActiveOptions]="{ exact: true }"
    >Products</a
  >
```

Nested Routes

Nested routes allow you to define subordinate routes that are dependent on a parent route.

```typescript
import { Routes } from
'@angular/router';
import { HomeComponent } from
'./pages/home/home.component';
import { NotFoundComponent } from
'./pages/not-found/not-found.component';
import { AddProductComponent } from
'./pages/add-product/add-product.compone
nt';
import { authGuard } from
'./guards/authGuard';
import { ProductsComponent } from
'./pages/products/products.component';
import { ProductsResolver } from
'./pages/resolvers/products.resolver';
import { ProductDetailsComponent } from
'./pages/product-details/product-details
.component';
import { ReviewsComponent } from
'./components/reviews/reviews.component'
;
import { VariationsComponent } from
'./components/variations/variations.comp
onent';
import { RatesComponent } from
'./components/rates/rates.component';

export const routes: Routes = [
  { path: '', redirectTo: 'home',
pathMatch: 'full' },
  {
```

```typescript
    path: 'home',
    component: HomeComponent,
    data: {
      title: 'Home Page',
      breadcrumb: 'Home',
      config: { theme: 'light', layout:
'default' },
    },
  },
  {
    path: 'products',
    component: ProductsComponent,
    resolve: {
      products: ProductsResolver,
    },
  },
  {
    path: 'products/:id',
    component: ProductDetailsComponent,
    children: [
      { path: '', redirectTo: 'rates',
pathMatch: 'full' },
      { path: 'variations', component:
VariationsComponent },
      { path: 'rates', component:
RatesComponent },
      { path: 'reviews', component:
ReviewsComponent },
    ],
  },
  {
```

```
    path: 'add-product',
    component: AddProductComponent,
    canActivate: [authGuard],
  },
  { path: 'not-found', component:
NotFoundComponent },
  {
    path: '**',
    redirectTo: 'not-found',
  },
];
```

The product detail page has three subpages, and the
rates page has been set up as the default subpage.
The functionality is very simple. Within your product
detail page, you add links for subordinate routes. If you
add links without the slash "/" at the beginning, they
become relative to the current path.
You need to add another <router-outlet /> where the
subordinate components should be rendered.
Your product detail page will then look similar to this
one:

```
<p>product-details works!</p>

<a
routerLink="variations">Variations</a>
<a routerLink="rates">Rates</a>
<a routerLink="reviews">Reviews</a>

<router-outlet />
```

Do not forget to import the `RouterModule` in your standalone component.

Scroll Position Restoration

If you have finished reading the content and are now at the end of the page and have clicked on one of the application links to go to another page. You will notice that Angular loads the new route, but you are still at the bottom of the page. If you want to go to the top every time you visit a new page, you should explicitly configure this in the **app.config.ts** when you provide the router. This is how it works.

```
import { ApplicationConfig,
provideZoneChangeDetection } from
'@angular/core';
import {
  InMemoryScrollingFeature,
  InMemoryScrollingOptions,
  provideRouter,
  withInMemoryScrolling,
} from '@angular/router';

import { routes } from './app.routes';

const scrollConfig:
InMemoryScrollingOptions = {
  scrollPositionRestoration: 'top',
  anchorScrolling: 'enabled',
```

```typescript
};
const inMemoryScrollingFeature:
InMemoryScrollingFeature =
  withInMemoryScrolling(scrollConfig);

export const appConfig:
ApplicationConfig = {
  providers: [
    provideZoneChangeDetection({
eventCoalescing: true }),
    provideRouter(routes,
inMemoryScrollingFeature),
  ],
};
```

Router Events

Router events are a series of events that the Angular
router emits during the navigation process. By
subscribing to these events, you can implement
functions such as load indicators, error handling and
analytical tracking.
In this example, I read the current URL after the
navigation event is completed. I can then use that URL
to highlight the active menu item or save it as part of the
analytics processing or whatever.

```typescript
  ngOnInit(): void {
    this.router.events.subscribe((event:
any) => {
```

```
      if (event instanceof
NavigationEnd) {
        this.url = event.url;
      }
    });
  }
```

Router Tracing

`withDebugTracing` **you will see detailed information about routing events to the console.**

```
import { ApplicationConfig,
provideZoneChangeDetection } from
'@angular/core';
import {
  InMemoryScrollingFeature,
  InMemoryScrollingOptions,
  provideRouter,
  withDebugTracing,
  withInMemoryScrolling,
} from '@angular/router';

import { routes } from './app.routes';

const scrollConfig:
InMemoryScrollingOptions = {
  scrollPositionRestoration: 'top',
  anchorScrolling: 'enabled',
};
```

```typescript
const inMemoryScrollingFeature:
InMemoryScrollingFeature =
  withInMemoryScrolling(scrollConfig);

export const appConfig:
ApplicationConfig = {
  providers: [
    provideZoneChangeDetection({
eventCoalescing: true }),
    provideRouter(routes,
inMemoryScrollingFeature,
withDebugTracing()),
  ],
};
```

Conclusion

Congratulations! You have read the book "Angular Routing: Everything you need to know". Now you are able to handle all routing scenarios with ease. Remember that learning Angular is an ongoing process. Practice makes perfect — build your own projects, experiment with the features you have learned, and delve into the extensive online resources.
Thank you for joining me in my exploration of Angular. I wish you the best of luck on your programming journey. Have fun programming and good luck with your applications!

Media Attributions

Modern annual report magazine page flyer a company
catalog
Image by starline on Freepik

Browsing online concept illustration
Image by storyset on Freepik

Don't miss out!

Receive an email when Abdelfattah Ragab publishes a new book. It's free and without obligation.

Also by Abdelfattah Ragab

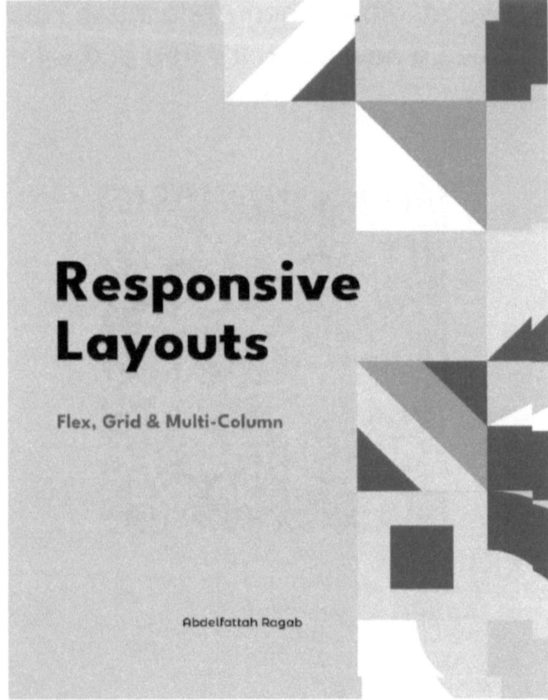

Responsive design is an approach to web design that ensures web pages render well on a variety of devices and screen sizes, from desktop monitors to mobile phones. The primary goal of responsive design is to provide an optimal viewing experience, making it easy for users to read and navigate the site with minimal resizing, panning, and scrolling.

About the Author

Abdelfattah Ragab is a professional software developer with more than 20 years of experience.
https://abdelfattah-ragab.com

About the Publisher

Abdelfattah Ragab is a highly qualified and experienced software developer with over 20 years of experience in the industry. Specializing in front-end development, Abdelfattah Ragab has a deep understanding of Angular, JavaScript, TypeScript, HTML and CSS. Read more at https://abdelfattah-ragab.com